THE CHINESE HOROSCOPES LIBRARY

RAM

KWOK MAN-HO

DORLING KINDERSLEY
LONDON • NEW YORK • STUTTGART

W9-AWF-056

A DORLING KINDERSLEY BOOK

Senior Editor — Sharon Lucas
Art Editor — Camilla Fox
Managing Editor — Krystyna Mayer
Managing Art Editor — Derek Coombes
DTP Designer — Doug Miller
Production Controller — Antony Heller
US Editor — Laaren Brown

Artworks: Danuta Mayer 4, 8, 11, 17, 27, 29, 31, 33, 35;
Giuliano Fornari 21; Studio Illibill 25; Jane Thomson; Sarah Ponder.

Special Photography by Steve Gorton. Thank you to The British Museum, Chinese Post Office, The Fan Museum – Hélène Alexander Collection, The Powell-Cotton Museum, and The Board of Trustees of the Victoria & Albert Museum.

Additional Photography: Eric Crichton, Michael Crockett, Jo Foord, Steve Gorton, Dave King, David Murray, Stephen Oliver, Clive Streeter.

Picture Credits: The Fan Museum – Hélène Alexander Collection 19tr, 22cr.

First American Edition, 1994
2 4 6 8 10 9 7 5 3

Published in the United States by Dorling Kindersley Publishing, Inc., 95 Madison Avenue, New York, New York 10016

Copyright © 1994
Dorling Kindersley Limited, London
Text copyright © 1994 ICOREC

ISBN 1-56458-607-3
Library of Congress Catalog Number 93-48006

Reproduced by GRB Editrice, Verona, Italy
Printed and bound in Hong Kong by Imago

Contents

INTRODUCING CHINESE HOROSCOPES

For thousands of years, the Chinese have used their astrology and religion to establish a harmony between people and the world around them.

The exact origins of the twelve animals of Chinese astrology – the Rat, Ox, Tiger, Rabbit, Dragon, Snake, Horse, Ram, Monkey, Rooster, Dog, and Pig – remain a mystery. Nevertheless, these animals are important in Chinese astrology. They are much more than general signposts to the year and to the possible good or bad times ahead for us all. The twelve animals of Chinese astrology are considered to be a reflection of the Universe itself.

YIN AND YANG SYMBOL
White represents the female force of yin, and black represents the masculine force of yang.

YIN AND YANG

The many differences in our natures, moods, health, and fortunes reflect the wider changes within the Universe. The Chinese believe that

every single thing in the Universe is held in balance by the dynamic, cosmic forces of yin and yang. Yin is feminine, watery, and cool; the force of the Moon and the rain. Yang is masculine, solid, and hot; the force of the Sun and the Earth. According to ancient Chinese belief, the concentrated essences of yin and yang became the four seasons, and the scattered essences of yin and yang became the myriad creatures that are found on Earth.

The twelve animals of Chinese astrology are all associated with either yin or yang. The forces of yin rise as Winter approaches. These forces decline with the warmth of Spring, when yang begins to assert itself. Even in the course of a normal day, yin and yang are at work, constantly changing and balancing. These forces also naturally rise and fall within us all.

Everyone has their own internal balance of yin and yang. This affects our tempers, ambitions, and health. We also respond to the changes of weather, to the environment, and to the people who surround us.

THE FIVE ELEMENTS

All that we can touch, taste, or see is divided into five basic types or elements – wood, fire, earth, gold, and water. Everything in the Universe can be linked to one of these elements.

For example, the element earth is linked to four animals – the Ox, Dragon, Ram, and Dog. This element is also linked to the color yellow, sweet-tasting food, and the

emotion of desire. The activity of these various elements indicates the fortune that may befall us.

AN INDIVIDUAL DISCOVERY

Chinese astrology can help you balance your yin and yang. It can also tell you which element you are, and the colors, tastes, parts of the body, or emotions that are linked to your particular sign. Your fortune can be prophesied according to the year, month, day, and hour in which you were born. You can identify the type of people to whom you are attracted, and the career that will suit your character. You can understand your changes of mood, your reactions to other places and to other people. In essence, you can start to discover what makes you an individual.

DIVINATION STICKS
Another ancient and popular method of Chinese fortune-telling is using special divination sticks to obtain a specific reading from prediction books.

CASTING YOUR HOROSCOPE

The Chinese calendar is based on the movement of the Moon, unlike the calendar used in the Western world, which is based on the movement of the Sun.

Before you begin to cast your Chinese horoscope, check your year of birth on the chart on pages 44 to 45. Check particularly carefully if you were born in the early months of the year. The Chinese year does not usually begin until January or February, and you might belong to the previous Chinese year. For example, if you were born in 1961 you might assume that you were born in the Year of the Ox. However, if your birthday falls before February 15 you belong to the previous Chinese year, which is the Year of the Rat.

THE SIXTY-YEAR CYCLE

The Chinese measure the passing of time by cycles of sixty years. The twelve astrological animals appear five times during the sixty-year cycle, and they appear in a slightly different form every time. For example, if you were born in 1943

you are a Ram in a Flock of Sheep, but if you were born in 1955, you are a Ram Respected by Others.

MONTHS, DAYS, AND HOURS

The twelve lunar months of the Chinese calendar do not correspond exactly with the twelve Western calendar months. This is because Chinese months are lunar, whereas Western months are solar. Chinese months are normally twenty-nine to thirty days long, and every three to four years an extra month is added to keep approximately in step with the Western year.

One Chinese hour is equal to two Western hours, and the twelve Chinese hours correspond to the twelve animal signs.

The year, month, day, and hour of birth are the keys to Chinese astrology. Once you know them, you can start to unlock your personal Chinese horoscope.

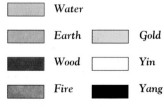

Water

Earth

Wood

Fire

Gold

Yin

Yang

CHINESE ASTROLOGICAL WHEEL
In the center of the wheel is the yin and yang symbol. It is surrounded by the Chinese astrological character linked to each animal. The band of color indicates your element, and the outer ring reveals whether you are yin or yang.

· RAM ·
MYTHS AND LEGENDS

The Jade Emperor, heaven's ruler, asked to see the Earth's twelve most interesting animals. When they arrived, he was impressed by the Ram's loveliness, and awarded it eighth place.

The Ram is a symbol of filial piety, because it kneels when it suckles from its mother. It also represents the male principle, yang – the Chinese word for sheep. The distinction between sheep and goats in the Far East was often fairly blurred, with goats being known as "sheep of the mountains." In Tibet and Mongolia, nomadic tribes buried sheep bones in the ground in Winter, in the belief that the earth would be fruitful in spring and lambs would be born. According to Chinese legend, five magicians met in the city of Canton in South China. Each magician rode a ram, and each ram carried a stalk of grain in its mouth.

HAN DYNASTY RAM

This earthenware ram is colored with a lead glaze. It is Chinese, from the Han dynasty (25–220).

The stalks of grain were presented to the local people with the wish that they should never suffer from want or famine. The magicians then disappeared, and the rams turned to stone. Even today, Canton is still sometimes called the City of Rams.

THE RAM AND THE TIGER

Long ago, a ram wandered into a deep forest. At first he felt quite happy, because there was plenty of fresh grass to eat. But soon the ram had eaten all the sweet grass, and the trees closed around him. The foolish ram was utterly lost, but kept

This beautiful bronze vessel is in the form of two rams. It dates from the Shang dynasty (1200BC–1001BC).

walking into the heart of the forest, feeling very frightened indeed. Suddenly, a vast, terrifying tiger leaped out from behind a great tree and grabbed the ram by the neck. Thinking that his end was nigh, the ram thought very quickly.

"How dare you attack me!" said the ram. The tiger was thoroughly surprised by this outburst and dropped the ram on the ground, but still held him with his huge, clawed foot. "What do you mean?" asked the tiger. "You are just a silly ram who will make a nice lunch for me. Why on earth should I not eat you?"

"How little you know," said the ram. "I have just been appointed King of All the Animals by the Jade Emperor himself." The tiger looked skeptical. "I haven't heard anything about this," he said.

"You must be the only animal that hasn't," said the ram defiantly. "If you don't believe me, just walk along behind me and watch how the other animals react to my presence." The tiger did as the ram suggested. When the animals of the forest saw the ram with the tiger walking behind it, they fled, fearing the tiger's strength and ferocity. But the tiger believed that it was the ram that scared the animals away. He acknowledged the ram as the King of All the Animals and gave him his freedom.

· RAM ·
PERSONALITY

Gentle and amiable, the Ram appreciates the fine, creative things in life. It is sensitive to its environment and is the most tranquil of the twelve Chinese animals.

You are the most mild-mannered and nervous of the animal signs. You have the imagination to transform your surroundings, and it is important for you to surround yourself with beauty.

MOTIVATION

Financial gain, power, and prestige do not hold great interest for you, but you will need financial backing to pursue life's creative pleasures. Once this security has been provided, you are content and will try to maintain your position at all costs.

THE INNER RAM

At heart you want to live in a peaceful world. You do not make demands on others, and neither do you want them to make any demands on you.

There is a strong spiritual side to your nature. You are easily touched by others' suffering and need freedom to follow your instincts.

THREE JADE RAMS

A Chinese artist or calligrapher would have used these three jade rams as a brush rest in the 17th century.

LUCK ON A PLATE

This Chinese porcelain plate is from the second half of the 16th century. It depicts three rams, which are auspicious symbols in Chinese mythology.

Although you have a retiring nature, you are charming and good company. You are a natural daydreamer and tend to need plenty of protection and guidance. Confrontation is anathema to you, and you dislike gossip. The positive sides of people's characters interest you far more than the negative, and you are sympathetic and conciliatory. Your hesitant nature can be frustrating, and your unpunctuality can be irritating. When you are criticized or stymied, you tend to become sulky and defensive, and mull over these supposed slights.

You never intend to be hurtful, and if you wound someone, it is invariably the result of your thoughtlessness or daydreaming, rather than any malicious intent. In emotional affairs you are open, loving, and affectionate, but you always need to feel protected and accepted for what you are.

You could never be accused of being the most conventional or responsible of parents, but your relaxed, creative nature is highly appealing to children.

THE RAM CHILD

The young Ram is a timid creature. It needs a peaceful environment and sensitive handling to stimulate and reveal its creative spirit.

· RAM ·
LOVE

The Ram is a sensitive creature and is ruled by its sympathies and feelings. It is demanding in love, but is willing to give everything, especially its heart.

You are careful not to reveal your emotions until you are sure they are reciprocated, and it is very important that your partner be faithful and protective. Although you are always adaptable, it is essential for your partner to fulfill your material and spiritual needs. Sometimes you may appear to be emotionally grasping, but once you feel secure you should feel able to give more of yourself.

You are affectionate, optimistic, and rarely anxious or jealous. In any case, you expect your partner to accept your faults.

Ideally, you are suited to the Rabbit or the Pig. You share the Rabbit's love of tranquillity, and its affection, patience, and organizational skills complement your imaginative nature. Your creativity and love of serenity also appeal to the Pig, and you will happily allow it to enjoy its own personal space.

You share a sense of independence with the Horse and enjoy its unpredictability. Your humor and sense of the unusual react well with

GODDESS OF LOVE
Kuan Yin is a powerful figure in Chinese mythology. Once a male Buddhist deity, she is now known as the goddess of mercy, and as Sung-tzu, the giver of children.

CHINESE COMPATIBILITY WHEEL

Find your animal sign, then look for the animals that share its background color – the Ram has a green background and is most compatible with the Pig and the Rabbit. The symbol in the center of the wheel represents double happiness.

the Monkey's vivacity, but beware of becoming too dependent. You may enjoy yourself with another Ram, but you will both find it hard to deal with life's practicalities. The Snake appreciates your love of art and, like you, favors an easy, relaxed lifestyle. The Dragon will give you plenty of encouragement, but it may be upset if it does not receive your unlimited adoration in return.

ORCHID

In China, the orchid, or Lan Hua, is an emblem of love and beauty. It is also a fertility symbol and represents many offspring.

A stable relationship with the Ox, Dog, Rooster, or Rat could be difficult to sustain. This is because your musings and dreams are in direct contrast to the Ox's stability and practicality; your nervousness could prove too much for the Dog's own anxieties; and the Rooster may require more attention and moral support than you are able to give. The Rat is likely to find you frustrating and may be unable to provide you with the emotional support that you need.

· RAM ·
CAREER

The Ram is very sensitive to the politics and pressures within its working environment and instinctively avoids getting itself involved in professional confrontations.

Bronze paperweight

JEWELED RAM
This ancient Chinese bronze ram paperweight is decorated with precious jewels. Perhaps it was made by a Ram, for the Ram has a natural aptitude for skilled handicraft work.

Script

LITERARY PURSUITS
The Ram has a lively, fertile imagination and needs sufficient space to express itself. A literary career suits the Ram well, and it has the talent to be a poet, scholar, advertising copywriter, or author. It is a conscientious creature and is happiest when it feels that it is successfully pursuing its own interests.

Marbled fountain pens

ARTIST

The freedom and creativity of the artist's life often appeals to the Ram. An artist painted this Chinese fan in the 19th century. The fan depicts an often dramatized scene from the 14th-century romance Shui Hu Chuan, or The Water Margin.

Chinese fan

Tap shoes

PERFORMING ARTIST

The Ram is motivated primarily by the desire to make the most of its talents. This single-minded approach is vital for the performing artist's work.

THEATRICAL WORK

The theater is an extremely conducive environment for the Ram. It likes to be involved with like-minded people in the creation of a piece of theater, whether as a playwright, performer, or technician.

Spotlight

HEALTH

Yin and yang are in a continual state of flux within the body. Good health is dependent upon the balance of yin and yang being constantly harmonious.

There is a natural minimum and maximum level of yin and yang in the human body. The body's energy is known as ch'i and is a yang force. The movement of ch'i in the human body is complemented by the movement of blood, which is a yin force. The very slightest displacement of the balance of yin or yang in the body can quickly lead to poor health and sickness.

LINGCHIH FUNGUS
The fungus shown in this detail from a Ch'ing dynasty bowl is the "immortal" lingchih fungus, which symbolizes longevity.

LICORICE
Emperor Shen-nung is reputed to have used this nontoxic herb medicinally in China five thousand years ago.

Yang illness can be cured by yin treatment, and yin illness can be cured by yang treatment. Everybody has their own individual balance of yin and yang. It is likely that a hot-tempered person will have strong yang forces, and that a peaceful person will have strong yin forces. Your nature is identified with your health, and before Chinese medicine can be prescribed, your moods have to be carefully taken into account. A balance of joy, anger, sadness, happiness, worry, pensiveness, and fear must always be maintained. This balance is known in China as the Harmony of the Seven Sentiments.

Born in the Year of the Ram, you are associated with the element earth. This element is linked with the spleen, pancreas, stomach, muscles, and mouth. These are the parts of the human body that are most relevant to the pattern of your health. You are also associated with the emotion of desire and with sweet-tasting food.

The herb licorice (*Glycyrrhiza glabra*) is associated with your astrological sign. It is one of the most frequently prescribed herbs in Chinese medicine and is prescribed to restore ch'i and to treat the spleen, sore throats, coughs, and food or drug poisoning. Licorice root can be ground and taken as a powder or pill, or boiled or soaked in water, with the resulting liquid being used to bathe the body.

Chinese medicine is highly specific; therefore, never take licorice or any other herb unless you are following professional advice from a fully qualified Chinese or Western doctor.

ASTROLOGY AND ANATOMY
Your element, earth, is associated with the digestive system. The stomach is a yang organ, and the pancreas, behind the stomach, is a yin organ.

· RAM ·
LEISURE

The Ram has a dreamy nature and prefers to be left alone to pursue its creative spirit. It is happiest in a harmonious, tranquil environment.

Artist's oil paints

ART

The Ram is an artistic creature and enjoys the "hands-on" nature of painting, particularly with oils. Although the Ram is not overly interested in possessions, it does derive pleasure from beautiful, individually crafted objects, such as this finely painted fan from 19th-century China.

Chinese fan

Artist's paintbrushes

HOME COMFORTS

Exquisite home furnishings, such as this traditional Regency dining chair and carved wooden chandelier, will delight any Ram.

Carved chandelier

Dining chair

Shang dynasty ram

YOGA

The stress of organizing events, or of competitive hobbies, makes the Ram recoil. It derives the most satisfaction from solitary pursuits, and the physical and mental exercise of yoga suit its temperament well.

Yoga mat

SHANG RAM

This Chinese bronze ram is from the Shang dynasty (c. 1200–1001BC). It is unfortunate that its legs are not well defined, because the Ram has an aversion to being restricted in any way.

SYMBOLISM

*In Chinese astrology, each of the twelve animals is linked
with a certain food, direction, color, emotion, association,
and symbol.*

**Chinese yellow-ground
medallion bowl**

COLOR

*In china, fertile earth has a yellow huye. Yellow
was the imperial color, worn by the emperor as
the First Son of the Earth. The color yellow is
also linked with the Ram. This Ch'ing dynasty
yellow-ground medallion bowl depicts the Ram
in a late winter scene.*

FOOD

*There are five tastes according to
Chinese astrology – salty, acrid,
bitter, sweet, and sour. Sweet foods,
such as cashews, are associated with
the Ram.*

Cashews

Section of a
map of Rome

Antique
Chinese
compass

DIRECTION

The Chinese compass points south, whereas the Western compass points north. The Chinese compass has an extra direction, the center, which is the Ram's direction.

ASSOCIATION

The capital city and its life are linked with the Ram.

SYMBOL

The Ram's symbol is the plumb line, which is used to measure the depth of water.

Plumb line

EMOTION

Desire is the emotion that is connected with the Ram.

*Baby
expressing
desire*

RAM RESPECTED BY OTHERS

~ 1955 2015 ~

Life is not particularly easy for this Ram, but it still manages to earn the respect of others. It achieves its successes through its own substantial efforts.

Although you may sometimes feel that your life is full of potential, it usually requires great personal effort for it to be realized.

YOUTH
During your school years, at the beginning of your career, and in the early stages of your committed relationship, you may experience some difficulties.

Ultimately, all these areas of your life should prove rewarding, because you are the Ram Respected by Others. However, you will probably not be particularly wealthy or lucky, but through hard work and careful management of your resources, you should certainly thrive.

It is natural for a Ram to want to buck against any system. You tend to be easily frustrated by the rules and regulations that seem to hem you in. Try to remember that excessive

reactions often cause difficulties and problems for you, and should always be avoided. It is probably best for you to be honest and open about your frustrations, but in a totally nonthreatening way. This is likely to stand you in good stead and should help you toward a successful and prosperous old age.

CAREER
Rams often like to flirt with the idea of being their own bosses and may even want to run their own businesses. However, there may be greater benefits and advantages to staying within a larger system.

Most Rams are prone to fret and worry about relatively minor issues and can work themselves into a state of near frenzy without too much effort. Perhaps you may find that being your own boss is significantly harder work than you originally

Ram Respected by Others

thought – not only might you have to find your own capital, but you may also have to discover new resources of physical and mental energy.

FAMILY
Your family will always be important to you, but unfortunately they are not often able to be particularly useful or helpful.

In order to avoid pain and disappointment, it is best to keep away from situations in which you have to rely on your family for

financial, or even emotional, support. This applies particularly to your siblings and to your parents.

RELATIONSHIPS
When choosing a partner, try to find someone who can be both calm and supportive. Ideally, your partner should be willing and able to put your anxieties and frustrations into a sensible perspective. Hopefully, you will be able to find a balance together, which will allow you to enjoy a successful and happy life.

LONELY RAM

~ 1907 1967 ~

All Rams resent authority and loathe being bound by petty regulations. They like to do things on their own, and consequently the Lonely Ram is full of character.

Going off on your own is a natural action for you, because you are associated with the sting of a bee. Symbolically, this suggests that you would rather make a forceful impact once, and then be gone, than wait and procrastinate. You make your mark on the world somehow, even if it causes some initial offense.

PERSONALITY

Since you are independent minded, you are likely to earn a reputation as someone who can be trusted. You enjoy a good argument, but your rebellious side is tempered by your consideration for others. You do not just score a point and depart – you like to follow up arguments instead.

However, being on your own can be difficult at times. Most Rams suffer from an innate sense of anxiety, and you can sometimes feel threatened and isolated.

Consequently, you are vulnerable to changes of mood. One day you can be "up," perhaps because you are excited about a new project. The very next day, however, you can be "down" because you may suddenly feel insecure about your ability.

These mood swings can be unnerving, but there is not much you can do about them. Just try not to be unduly alarmed, and make every attempt to keep them under control.

CAREER

Because you are invariably willing to take risks, you should find that you are successful in terms of material benefits or great job satisfaction.

FAMILY

Your love of life on the edge may mean that your family, especially your siblings, do not always appreciate you as much as you would

Lonely Ram

wish. This can lead to tense and awkward situations, which may need to be handled with care.

RELATIONSHIPS

Perhaps because you have tended to be single-minded, and have decided to concentrate your attentions on your own career and ventures, you are most likely to commit yourself to a long-term relationship later in life. This means that you will probably have your children when you are significantly older than most other parents. The delay should prove beneficial, because over the years you should find a balance between your career and your family's needs.

RAM RUNNING
ON THE MOUNTAIN

~ 1919 1979 ~

This is the Ram on its home territory. As a result, you are able to adapt yourself to most circumstances easily, and you seem to be comfortable in the oddest situations.

You are associated with the web of life, and consequently, always seem to fit in well with the general scheme of things. The Ram Running on the Mountain is a very auspicious sign, and you should be able to succeed at whatever you decide to do.

Because you are so infinitely adaptable, it is always likely to be very easy for you to live and work wherever you wish. Your innate Ram nature makes you more than willing to take responsibility for your own life, and your singlemindedness should invariably prove beneficial.

PERSONALITY

Your greatest qualities are your honesty and reliability. People know that they can trust you and expect you to say exactly what you mean, not necessarily what they might want to hear. Consequently, you are likely to have people's confidence and support, even when your life becomes difficult.

Physically, you always deport yourself well and are often known for your sartorial elegance.

CAREER

In situations that require debate, clarification, or even occasional confrontation, you tend to be quick to take the lead. Since you are generally esteemed as a person of integrity, people are always likely to pay more attention to you than they would to others.

You invariably earn the respect and friendship of your superiors through the combination of your enjoyable personality, impressive record of plain speaking, and thoughtful contribution to ideas and projects. Over the years, all these

Ram Running on the Mountain

valuable qualities should aid your successful rise through the ranks. You are a particularly fortunate Ram – it is highly likely that you will enjoy eventual positions of significant authority and power.

FRIENDSHIPS

You should be able to form strong and rewarding friendships with many people, for you are very good company. Your appearance can sometimes be deceptive, however. Often you may seem to be cheerful and relaxed, when you are actually quite tense and overwrought with anxieties and petty worries.

PROSPECTS

If you remain true to your essential personality, you should enjoy a comfortable life. You are likely to take virtually everything in your stride, even though there will be times when you, and you alone, know that under your calm and reassuring exterior lie nagging tensions and anxieties.

PROSPEROUS RAM

~ 1931 1991 ~

*Although the name of this Ram suggests great good fortune,
it is most likely to be the female Prosperous Ram who will
be able to live up to this optimistic title.*

Your potential for success and achievement is counterbalanced by your association with decline and sadness. Unfortunately, if you are an elder son born under the sign of the Prosperous Ram, you may find that your life is particularly difficult.

FEMALE CHARACTERISTICS
Because of the yin influence, the female Prosperous Ram can look forward to a prosperous life. Her drive to excel should find plenty of opportunity for expression. As a result, she has a strong spirit of idealism and optimism.

MALE CHARACTERISTICS
This spirit is also shared by the male, but because of the yang influence, he is frequently disappointed. He can seem hesitant when he tries to tackle demanding tasks, and this reticence is likely to impede his progress. It is

only much later in life that he is likely to have learned how to succeed. All male Prosperous Rams, and particularly those who are elder sons, are likely to experience problems with their relatives. An elder son may often find himself utterly opposed to his parents.

Most Prosperous Rams will have to endure many years of family arguing and wrangling. To avoid distress, perhaps you and your family should strive to achieve some distance and learn how to appreciate each other anew.

Never risk losing the ability to be honest about your feelings, but try to remember that other people have feelings, too.

RELATIONSHIPS
It is a Ram characteristic to dislike conflict, and you are no exception. You are very forgiving, and every

Prosperous Ram

conceivable attempt is made by you to restore hurt or damaged relationships as soon as possible. These valuable traits should prove highly beneficial in your personal life. Your naturally giving, and forgiving, nature, should ensure a happy committed relationship of great mutual satisfaction.

PROSPECTS

Any Prosperous Ram is likely to find life a constant source of minor anxieties. However, with your innate forgiveness, you should emerge with your integrity intact and your relationships strengthened. This should ensure a stable and contented old age.

RAM IN A FLOCK OF SHEEP

~ 1943 2003 ~

As the only male in a flock of females, this Ram may seem to be in a lucky position, but unfortunately, being exposed often tends to bring its own problems.

Because you tend to stand out from other people, it is important for you to behave in an exemplary manner. This is given further emphasis by your association with correct behavior, which brings satisfaction and possibly reward.

PERSONALITY

As a Ram, you always run the risk, or perhaps use the advantage, of speaking your mind. You tend not to do the same as other people and always want to be in control of your own life. There is nothing wrong with these characteristics, but they can sometimes make you appear brusque and tactless.

You are prone to launch into a tirade or discourse without knowing all the facts, or without taking the feelings of others into proper account. Consequently, you are not always popular.

Beneath this rather rough exterior, however, is a very kind person. You do not mean to cause offense, and often go out of your way to help others and to care for them. Your strong charitable streak may lead you to work with people in need, but this is unlikely to bring you significant praise or reward.

Do not worry about this lack of recognition. Always remember that if you manage to keep your sharp tongue under firm control, you should become considerably more likable, and people will eventually learn to appreciate the warmer side of your personality.

YOUTH

Because of your slightly difficult personality, you are likely to find that your early years are not easy and that the way to success is a rough path to walk.

Ram in a Flock of Sheep

RELATIONSHIPS

Unfortunately, the early years of your committed relationship are also likely to be difficult. These years will inevitably consist of considerable upheaval and will involve learning to settle down with someone, to trust another person, and to appreciate and accept a different point of view.

It is important for you to choose a partner who will not be upset by the strength of your feelings, and who will encourage you to give vent to them instead. Once you have found your partner, make sure that you never take him or her for granted.

PROSPECTS

The combination of your brusque nature and your inclination to align yourself with the underprivileged may bring you many troubles. Beware of your manner, but never abandon your concern for the less fortunate. As time progresses, you should eventually be rewarded.

YOUR CHINESE
MONTH OF BIRTH

Find the table with your year of birth, and see where your birthday falls. For example, if you were born on August 30, 1955, you were born in Chinese month 7.

1 Your communication skills are excellent, but you must beware of arrogance. Success should be yours.

2 You are highly skilled and could rise to a very important position. Accept your good fortune.

3 You dislike taking orders, but you never wish to have full control. You are a trusted colleague.

4 You are a loner and work very hard. Your shyness can make you seem selfish – try to share more.

5 You are a dilettante and skip from one project to another. Try to find a patient, helpful partner.

6 You are popular and successful, and life should yield its riches without too much personal effort.

7 You are honorable and a trustworthy friend. These qualities will bring their own reward.

8 You are hardworking, fun, and determined, and should eventually be successful in life.

9 You are a perfectionist, but can be too harsh on yourself and on others. Learn to relax more.

10 You are very bright, but can be vindictive. To be happy, you will need to control your ruthlessness.

11 You have a strong, attractive personality, but are too fickle. Try to listen to other people's advice.

12 You can be compassionate and caring, and should control your ability to be selfish and ruthless.

* Some Chinese years contain double months:	
1919: Month 7	1955: Month 3
July 27 – Aug 24	March 24 – April 21
Aug 25 – Sept 23	April 22 – May 21
1979: Month 6	
June 24 – July 23	
July 24 – Aug 22	

1907	
Feb 13 – March 13	1
March 14 – April 12	2
April 13 – May 11	3
May 12 – June 10	4
June 11 – July 9	5
July 10 – Aug 8	6
Aug 9 – Sept 7	7
Sept 8 – Oct 6	8
Oct 7 – Nov 5	9
Nov 6 – Dec 4	10
Dec 5 – Jan 3 1908	11
Jan 4 – Feb 1	12

1919	
Feb 1 – March 1	1
March 2 – March 31	2
April 1 – April 29	3
April 30 – May 28	4
May 29 – June 27	5
June 28 – July 26	6
See double months box	7
Sept 24 – Oct 23	8
Oct 24 – Nov 21	9
Nov 22 – Dec 21	10
Dec 22 – Jan 20 1920	11
Jan 21 – Feb 19	12

1931	
Feb 17 – March 18	1
March 19 – April 17	2
April 18 – May 16	3
May 17 – June 15	4
June 16 – July 14	5
July 15 – Aug 13	6
Aug 14 – Sept 11	7
Sept 12 – Oct 10	8
Oct 11 – 9 Nov 10	9
Nov 10 – Dec 8	10
Dec 9 – Jan 7 1932	11
Jan 8 – Feb 5	12

1943	
Feb 5 – March 5	1
March 6 – April 4	2
April 5 – May 3	3
May 4 – June 2	4
June 3 – July 1	5
July 2 – July 31	6
Aug 1 – Aug 30	7
Aug 31 – Sept 28	8
Sept 29 – Oct 28	9
Oct 29 – Nov 26	10
Nov 27 – Dec 26	11
Dec 27 – Jan 24 1944	12

1955	
Jan 24 – Feb 21	1
Feb 22 – March 23	2
See double months box	3
May 22 – June 19	4
June 20 – July 18	5
July 19 – Aug 17	6
Aug 18 – Sept 15	7
Sept 16 – Oct 15	8
Oct 16 – Nov 13	9
Nov 14 – Dec 13	10
Dec 14 – Jan 12 1956	11
Jan 13 – Feb 11	12

1967	
Feb 9 – March 10	1
March 11 – April 9	2
April 10 – May 8	3
May 9 – June 7	4
June 8 – July 7	5
July 8 – Aug 5	6
Aug 6 – Sept 3	7
Sept 4 – Oct 3	8
Oct 4 – Nov 1	9
Nov 2 – Dec 1	10
Dec 2 – Dec 30	11
Dec 31 – Jan 29 1968	12

1979	
Jan 28 – Feb 26	1
Feb 27 – March 27	2
March 28 – April 25	3
April 26 – May 25	4
May 26 – June 23	5
See double months box	6
Aug 23 – Sept 20	7
Sept 21 – Oct 20	8
Oct 21 – Nov 19	9
Nov 20 – Dec 18	10
Dec 19 – Jan 17 1980	11
Jan 18 – Feb 15	12

1991	
Feb 15 – March 15	1
March 16 – April 14	2
April 15 – May 13	3
May 14 – June 11	4
June 12 – July 11	5
July 12 – Aug 9	6
Aug 10 – Sept 7	7
Sept 8 – Oct 7	8
Oct 8 – Nov 5	9
Nov 6 – Dec 5	10
Dec 6 – Jan 4 1992	11
Jan 5 – Feb 3	12

2003	
Feb 1 – March 2	1
March 3 – April 1	2
April 2 – April 30	3
May 1 – May 30	4
May 31 – June 29	5
June 30 – July 28	6
July 29 – Aug 27	7
Aug 28 – Sept 25	8
Sept 26 – Oct 24	9
Oct 25 – Nov 23	10
Nov 24 – Dec 22	11
Dec 23 – Jan 21 2004	12

YOUR CHINESE
DAY OF BIRTH

*Refer to the previous page to discover the beginning of your
Chinese month of birth, then use the chart below to
calculate your Chinese day of birth.*

If you were born on May 5, 1907, your birthday is in the month starting on April 13. Find 13 on the chart below. Using 13 as the first day, count the days until you reach the date of your birthday. (Remember that not all months contain 31 days.) You were born on day 23 of the Chinese month.

If you were born in a Chinese double month, simply count the days from the first date of the month that contains your birthday.

1	2	3	4	5	6	7
8	9	10	11	12	13	14
15	16	17	18	19	20	21
22	23	24	25	26	27	28
29	30	31				

DAY 1, 10, 19, OR 28
You are trustworthy and set high standards, but tend to rush your projects. Try to be cautious, and do not be too self-obsessed. You may receive unexpected money but must control your spending. You are suited to a career in the public sector or the arts.

DAY 2, 11, 20, OR 29
You are honest and popular. You need peace, but also require lively company. You are prone to outbursts of temper. You tend to enjoy life and make the most of your opportunities. You are suited to a literary or artistic career.

DAY 3, 12, 21, OR 30
You are quick-witted, but may appear to be difficult. As a result, people may be wary of being your friend. You have a disciplined character and fight for the truth. You are suited to careers that have a competitive element.

Day 4, 13, 22, or 31

You are very warmhearted, but also have a reserved attitude, which can sometimes make you appear unapproachable. If you try to be more outgoing and sociable, you should become more popular. You have a calm and patient manner, and are suited to a career as an academic or researcher.

Day 5, 14, or 23

Your fiery, obstinate nature can sometimes make it difficult for you to accept suggestions or opinions from others, and your stubbornness may lead to quarrels or problems. You should be lucky with money and may often use your profits to set up new projects. Your innate intelligence will enable you to cope with a demanding career.

Day 6, 15, or 24

You have an open, stable, and cheerful character, and enjoy an active social life. You are affectionate and emotional, and have a tendency to daydream. This can lead to confusion, and your eagerness to help others may be stifled by your indecision. Although you will never be wealthy, you should always have enough money.

Day 7, 16, or 25

You enjoy a certain amount of excitement in your life, but must learn to become more realistic and disciplined. Although you are a natural performer, you should beware of alienating your friends or colleagues. In your career, the opportunity to travel is more important to you than a good salary or a high standard of living.

Day 8, 17, or 26

You have very good judgment, but should not act too quickly. Your social skills may sometimes be lacking, and you may alienate other people, so try to be more tactful. You will experience poverty, but also wealth. Your calm and determined nature is combined with a free spirit, making you best suited to self-employment.

Day 9, 18, or 27

You are happy, optimistic, and warmhearted. You keep yourself busy and are rarely troubled by trivialities. Occasionally you quarrel unnecessarily with your friends, and it is important for you to learn to control your moods. You are particularly suited to a career as a sole owner or proprietor.

YOUR CHINESE
HOUR OF BIRTH

In Chinese time, one hour is equal to two Western hours.
Each Chinese double hour is associated with one of the
twelve astrological animals.

11 P.M. – 1 A.M. RAT HOUR
You are independent and have a hot temper. Try to think before you speak. Your thrifty nature will be useful in business and at home. You are willing to help those who are close to you, and they will return your support.

1 – 3 A.M. OX HOUR
Up to the age of twenty, your life could be difficult, but your fortunes are likely to improve after these troublesome years. In your career, be prepared to take a risk or to leave home during your youth to achieve your goals. You should enjoy a prosperous old age.

3 – 5 A.M. TIGER HOUR
You have a lively and creative nature, which may cause family arguments in your youth. Between the ages of twenty and forty you may have many problems. Luckily, your fortunes are likely to improve dramatically in your forties.

5 – 7 A.M. RABBIT HOUR
Your parents should be helpful, but your siblings may be your rivals. You may have to move away from home to achieve your full potential at work. Your committed relationship may take time to become settled, but you should get along much better with everyone after middle age.

7 – 9 A.M. DRAGON HOUR
You have a quick-witted, determined, and attractive nature. Your life will be busy, but you could sometimes be lonely. You should achieve a good standard of living. Try to curb your excessive self-confidence, for it could make working relationships difficult.

9 – 11 A.M. SNAKE HOUR

You have a talent for business and should find it easy to build your career and provide for your family. You have a very generous spirit and will gladly help your friends when they are in trouble. Unfortunately, family relationships are unlikely to run smoothly.

11 A.M. – 1 P.M. HORSE HOUR

You are active, clever, and obstinate. Try to listen to advice. You are fascinated with travel and with changing your life. Learn to control your extravagance, for it could lead to financial suffering.

1 – 3 P.M. RAM HOUR

Steady relationships with your family, friends, or partners are difficult, because you have an active nature. You are clever, but must not force your views on others. Your fortunes will be at their lowest in your middle age.

3 – 5 P.M. MONKEY HOUR

You earn and spend money easily. Your character is attractive, but frustrating, too. Sometimes your parents are not able to give you adequate moral support. Your committed relationship should be good, but do not brood over emotional problems for too long – if you do your career could suffer.

5 – 7 P.M. ROOSTER HOUR

In your teenage years you may have many arguments with your family. There could even be a family division, which should eventually be resolved. You are trustworthy, kind, and warmhearted, and never intend to hurt other people.

7 – 9 P.M. DOG HOUR

Your brave, capable, hard-working nature is ideally suited to self-employment, and the forecast for your career is excellent. Try to control your impatience and vanity. The quality of your life is far more important to you than the amount of money you have saved.

9 – 11 P.M. PIG HOUR

You are particularly skilled at manual work and always set yourself high standards. Although you are warmhearted, you do not like to surround yourself with too many friends. However, the people who are close to you have your complete trust. You can be easily upset by others, but are able to forgive and forget quickly.

YOUR FORTUNE IN OTHER ANIMAL YEARS

*The Ram's fortunes fluctuate during the twelve animal years.
It is best to concentrate on a year's positive aspects, and to
take care when faced with the seemingly negative.*

YEAR OF THE RAT
Success is most likely to
come from unexpected
sources in the Year of the
Rat, and you may also receive
considerable financial help. Your
emotional life should flourish, too.
You should be extremely happy in
this excellent year.

YEAR OF THE OX
Negative elements, such
as quarrels, arguments,
and strife, will tend
to dominate the Year of the Ox.
Unfortunately, there is little respite,
and you will have to endure these
major irritations when you are at
work, at home, and at leisure.

YEAR OF THE TIGER
You should make great
progress in your career
this year, and there are
likely to be large improvements in
your family life. However, you must
beware of succumbing to minor
accidents and illnesses.

YEAR OF THE RABBIT
This year, you will enjoy
success of a financial
nature. You are as
susceptible to accidents and illnesses
in the Year of the Rabbit as you were
last year; make sure that you take
sufficiently good care of your
physical and mental health.

YEAR OF THE DRAGON
There is no faulting your
hard work this year, but
unfortunately you will see
very little result for your efforts.
Whatever you try to do, and no
matter how hard you try, this is a
year when nothing seems to work
out to your advantage.

YEAR OF THE SNAKE

Your professional life should make steady, satisfactory progress in the Year of the Snake. If you motivate yourself to exploit the many opportunities that are offered to you this year, you should eventually be well rewarded.

YEAR OF THE HORSE

The underlying themes of the Year of the Horse are positivity, celebration, and happiness. Consequently, you can expect to enjoy yourself to the utmost at the many social events of the year. It is likely to be a time of great fun and success.

YEAR OF THE RAM

Although the Year of the Ram is your own year, it is generally an unsettled time. You will achieve the best results if you avoid rash behavior. Try to watch people and events carefully, then decide upon the correct course of action.

YEAR OF THE MONKEY

It may seem far too good to be true, but the Year of the Monkey is an extremely auspicious year for the Ram. Consequently, you should enjoy success in all areas of your life. Be sure to make the most of this excellent fortune.

YEAR OF THE ROOSTER

This is a year that is full of disagreements and quarrels. At times there will seem to be no escape, because you will have to cope with irritating disruptions in your home life and in your professional life, too.

YEAR OF THE DOG

Nothing seems to work out to your advantage during the Year of the Dog, and your family life is particularly likely to cause you problems. If you remain calm, however, these problems should resolve themselves.

YEAR OF THE PIG

This year may seem to be a continuation of the last — nothing is settled and everything is at odds. However, as long as you are careful and choose your friends wisely, you should achieve a degree of success in the Year of the Pig.

YOUR CHINESE
YEAR OF BIRTH

*Your astrological animal corresponds to the Chinese year of
your birth. It is the single most important key in the quest
to unlock your Chinese horoscope.*

Find your Western year of birth in
the left-hand column of the chart.
Your Chinese astrological animal is
on the same line as your year of birth
in the right-hand column of the
chart. If you were born in the
beginning of the year, check the

middle column of the chart carefully.
For example, if you were born in
1968, you might assume that you
belong to the Year of the Monkey.
However, if your birthday falls
before January 30, you actually
belong to the Year of the Ram.

1900	Jan 31 – Feb 18, 1901	Rat
1901	Feb 19 – Feb 7, 1902	Ox
1902	Feb 8 – Jan 28, 1903	Tiger
1903	Jan 29 – Feb 15, 1904	Rabbit
1904	Feb 16 – Feb 3, 1905	Dragon
1905	Feb 4 – Jan 24, 1906	Snake
1906	Jan 25 – Feb 12, 1907	Horse
1907	Feb 13 – Feb 1, 1908	Ram
1908	Feb 2 – Jan 21, 1909	Monkey
1909	Jan 22 – Feb 9, 1910	Rooster
1910	Feb 10 – Jan 29, 1911	Dog
1911	Jan 30 – Feb 17, 1912	Pig
1912	Feb 18 – Feb 5, 1913	Rat
1913	Feb 6 – Jan 25, 1914	Ox
1914	Jan 26 – Feb 13, 1915	Tiger
1915	Feb 14 – Feb 2, 1916	Rabbit
1916	Feb 3 – Jan 22, 1917	Dragon

1917	Jan 23 – Feb 10, 1918	Snake
1918	Feb 11 – Jan 31, 1919	Horse
1919	Feb 1 – Feb 19, 1920	Ram
1920	Feb 20 – Feb 7, 1921	Monkey
1921	Feb 8 – Jan 27, 1922	Rooster
1922	Jan 28 – Feb 15, 1923	Dog
1923	Feb 16 – Feb 4, 1924	Pig
1924	Feb 5 – Jan 23, 1925	Rat
1925	Jan 24 – Feb 12, 1926	Ox
1926	Feb 13 – Feb 1, 1927	Tiger
1927	Feb 2 – Jan 22, 1928	Rabbit
1928	Jan 23 – Feb 9, 1929	Dragon
1929	Feb 10 – Jan 29, 1930	Snake
1930	Jan 30 – Feb 16, 1931	Horse
1931	Feb 17 – Feb 5, 1932	Ram
1932	Feb 6 – Jan 25, 1933	Monkey
1933	Jan 26 – Feb 13, 1934	Rooster

1934	Feb 14 – Feb 3, 1935	Dog	1971	Jan 27 – Feb 14, 1972	Pig
1935	Feb 4 – Jan 23, 1936	Pig	1972	Feb 15 – Feb 2, 1973	Rat
1936	Jan 24 – Feb 10, 1937	Rat	1973	Feb 3 – Jan 22, 1974	Ox
1937	Feb 11 – Jan 30, 1938	Ox	1974	Jan 23 – Feb 10, 1975	Tiger
1938	Jan 31 – Feb 18, 1939	Tiger	1975	Feb 11 – Jan 30, 1976	Rabbit
1939	Feb 19 – Feb 7, 1940	Rabbit	1976	Jan 31 – Feb 17, 1977	Dragon
1940	Feb 8 – Jan 26, 1941	Dragon	1977	Feb 18 – Feb 6, 1978	Snake
1941	Jan 27 – Feb 14, 1942	Snake	1978	Feb 7 – Jan 27, 1979	Horse
1942	Feb 15 – Feb 4, 1943	Horse	1979	Jan 28 – Feb 15, 1980	Ram
1943	Feb 5 – Jan 24, 1944	Ram	1980	Feb 16 – Feb 4, 1981	Monkey
1944	Jan 25 – Feb 12, 1945	Monkey	1981	Feb 5 – Jan 24, 1982	Rooster
1945	Feb 13 – Feb 1, 1946	Rooster	1982	Jan 25 – Feb 12, 1983	Dog
1946	Feb 2 – Jan 21, 1947	Dog	1983	Feb 13 – Feb 1, 1984	Pig
1947	Jan 22 – Feb 9, 1948	Pig	1984	Feb 2 – Feb 19, 1985	Rat
1948	Feb 10 – Jan 28, 1949	Rat	1985	Feb 20 – Feb 8, 1986	Ox
1949	Jan 29 – Feb 16, 1950	Ox	1986	Feb 9 – Jan 28, 1987	Tiger
1950	Feb 17 – Feb 5, 1951	Tiger	1987	Jan 29 – Feb 16, 1988	Rabbit
1951	Feb 6 – Jan 26, 1952	Rabbit	1988	Feb 17 – Feb 5, 1989	Dragon
1952	Jan 27 – Feb 13, 1953	Dragon	1989	Feb 6 – Jan 26, 1990	Snake
1953	Feb 14 – Feb 2, 1954	Snake	1990	Jan 27 – Feb 14, 1991	Horse
1954	Feb 3 – Jan 23, 1955	Horse	1991	Feb 15 – Feb 3, 1992	Ram
1955	Jan 24 – Feb 11, 1956	Ram	1992	Feb 4 – Jan 22, 1993	Monkey
1956	Feb 12 – Jan 30, 1957	Monkey	1993	Jan 23 – Feb 9, 1994	Rooster
1957	Jan 31 – Feb 17, 1958	Rooster	1994	Feb 10 – Jan 30, 1995	Dog
1958	Feb 18 – Feb 7, 1959	Dog	1995	Jan 31 – Feb 18, 1996	Pig
1959	Feb 8 – Jan 27, 1960	Pig	1996	Feb 19 – Feb 6, 1997	Rat
1960	Jan 28 – Feb 14, 1961	Rat	1997	Feb 7 – Jan 27, 1998	Ox
1961	Feb 15 – Feb 4, 1962	Ox	1998	Jan 28 – Feb 15, 1999	Tiger
1962	Feb 5 – Jan 24, 1963	Tiger	1999	Feb 16 – Feb 4, 2000	Rabbit
1963	Jan 25 – Feb 12, 1964	Rabbit	2000	Feb 5 – Jan 23, 2001	Dragon
1964	Feb 13 – Feb 1, 1965	Dragon	2001	Jan 24 – Feb 11, 2002	Snake
1965	Feb 2 – Jan 20, 1966	Snake	2002	Feb 12 – Jan 31, 2003	Horse
1966	Jan 21 – Feb 8, 1967	Horse	2003	Feb 1 – Jan 21, 2004	Ram
1967	Feb 9 – Jan 29, 1968	Ram	2004	Jan 22 – Feb 8, 2005	Monkey
1968	Jan 30 – Feb 16, 1969	Monkey	2005	Feb 9 – Jan 28, 2006	Rooster
1969	Feb 17 – Feb 5, 1970	Rooster	2006	Jan 29 – Feb 17, 2007	Dog
1970	Feb 6 – Jan 26, 1971	Dog	2007	Feb 18 – Feb 6, 2008	Pig